The
SHADY
DEAL

**Tales of Cleverness
and Cunning**

RETOLD BY BRENDA PARKES AND
JANET STOTT-THORNTON

Retold by Brenda Parkes and Janet Stott-Thornton
Illustrated by Dominique Falla, Peter Foster, Kelvin Hawley,
    Marina McAllan, and Peter Shaw
Designed by Marina Messiha and Peter Shaw

Published by **Mimosa Publications Pty Ltd**
PO Box 779, Hawthorn 3122, Australia
© 1995 Mimosa Publications Pty Ltd
All rights reserved

Literacy 2000 is a Trademark registered in the
United States Patent and Trademark Office.

Distributed in the United States of America by

Rigby
A Division of Reed Elsevier Inc.
500 Coventry Lane
Crystal Lake, IL 60014
800-822-8661

Distributed in Canada by
    PRENTICE HALL GINN
    1870 Birchmount Road
    Scarborough
    Ontario M1P 2J7

99 98 97 96
10 9 8 7 6 5 4 3 2
Printed in Hong Kong through Bookbuilders Ltd

ISBN 0 7327 1578 4

CONTENTS

COMING CLEAN

Long ago, there lived a wise judge. He was known far and wide throughout the land, and respected for his wisdom and fairness.

One night, in a town not far from where the judge lived, there was a robbery – some precious jewels were stolen. The town officials quickly arrested a lot of suspects and questioned them all thoroughly. But no matter how many questions were asked, it was impossible to determine which of the suspects was the guilty one. Finally, the officials became so frustrated that they called on the wise judge.

The judge made *no* attempt to question the suspects. Instead, he announced, "In the old temple upon the highest hill, there is an ancient gong. It will tell us who stole the jewels."

So the gong was brought down from the temple and hung in the square. Late that night, the judge went to the square. With him he carried a fire pot, which he lit and then placed under the gong. Black smoke rose up from the fire pot and the judge watched

closely until the fire finally died down. Then he carefully placed a cover over the gong and went home to bed.

The next morning, the judge summoned the suspects to the square. Many people came to watch. They were eager to see how the gong would reveal the culprit. The crowd listened in silence as the judge spoke.

"This ancient gong has special powers," he said, in a slow, dignified voice. "Innocent people may touch it and it won't make a sound, but if a guilty thief so much as brushes a finger lightly against it, it will boom so loudly that the mountains will tremble."

A murmur went through the crowd. The suspects standing before the ancient gong rubbed their hands nervously.

The judge continued. "Upon my command, each of you shall step forward in turn, put your hand under the cover, and touch the gong."

Then, as the judge gestured to each one, the suspects stepped forward and reached under the cover. Time after time the gong made no sound. Then, as the last suspect stepped forward, a hush came over the square as the people waited to hear the ancient gong boom and the mountains tremble. Surely this man must be the thief. But when the last suspect reached under the cover, the gong made no sound at all. What could it mean? The crowd was restless and uneasy. Could the wise judge have made a mistake? The suspects looked puzzled, too.

10

Then the judge spoke again. "This one is the thief," he said, pointing confidently to one of the suspects.

The accused man began to protest. So too did the crowd. How could this man be the thief if the gong had not sounded?

"Let him go!" they shouted.

But the judge remained calm and certain. He ordered the cover to be lifted. Then the crowd saw that the ancient gong was covered in black soot, except for the places where the suspects' hands had touched it.

"Look," said the judge. "Each man who touched the ancient gong has black soot on his hand. Only one suspect has clean hands. Only one of the suspects was too afraid to touch the gong, lest it sound out his guilt. This man is your thief."

The crowd cheered. At last, the thief had been identified. The innocent suspects could be freed and the jewels would be returned.

And, from that day on, the people were more certain than ever before that the judge was one of the wisest people in all the land.

THE JACKAL AND THE CROCODILE

A long time ago, and a very long way from here, there was a jackal who lived in a house in the jungle. Now, close by the house was a river, and every morning, the jackal went down to the water's edge to catch his breakfast. Crabs snatched straight from the water were the jackal's favorite food. They were so delicious that he didn't mind occasionally having his paws nipped to catch them.

One morning, as the jackal was fishing for crabs, he noticed a long dark shadow in the water. He felt a prickly shiver along his back, for he was almost certain that it was the ferocious steel-jaw crocodile. This beast had not been seen in the jungle for many years, but the jackal had heard many frightening stories of animals disappearing forever into this croc's strong jaws.

But before he could so much as yelp or jump to safety, the jackal felt something sharp grab at his leg – something much bigger and stronger than the claw of a crab, and it held him tight.

Now, the jackal was clever, and he thought quickly. Instead of crying out in pain and fright and trying to pull away, the jackal began to laugh. He laughed and laughed.

"He he hee, what a good joke this is! I bet that old croc thinks he's got something good to eat. Just look at him with that tree branch in his mouth. How silly he looks! He he hee!"

Well, the ferocious steel-jaw crocodile was not just any crocodile. He was big and old and mean, and he hated to look a fool.

"I'll not be seen with a mere branch in my powerful jaws," he thought, and he let go very quickly.

The jackal sprang up onto the riverbank, hardly wounded at all.

"Thank you very much, Mister Crocodile!" he shouted with great glee, and some considerable relief. "I hope you do catch something to eat – but I doubt whether you are clever enough." And with that he ran away into the jungle to warn all his friends of the danger at the river.

The crocodile reared up in the water in his anger. Crashing down again, he caused a great wave to wash over the riverbank. A flock of birds in the tree above flew away in alarm.

"Thinks he's tricked me, does he? I'll have him for breakfast yet." And the crocodile sank down into the muddied water to await the jackal's return.

The jackal took such care to warn all the animals in the jungle about the crocodile that not a single animal went down to the river for a whole week. No one wanted to become the croc's next meal. But it wasn't long before the jackal missed his favorite food and thought about returning to the river.

At first, he stood a safe distance from the water's edge. The jackal was cautious as well as clever, and although he could see no sign of the croc, he knew that it could be lurking just beneath the surface.

"Oh dear," said the jackal loudly. "There are no crabs here. They usually make lots of bubbles, and there are no bubbles in the river today. I'll have to go away and look for something else to eat." And then he waited.

The crocodile was hiding among some reeds. He heard the jackal and he smiled a crocodile smile.

"Now it's my turn to outwit that cheeky jackal," he thought. "If I slide down under the water and blow some bubbles, he will come to the water's edge to catch crabs. I'll have him for breakfast after all."

But, of course, the crocodile was wrong. As soon as the jackal saw the bubbles, he jumped in the air and laughed like a laughing hyena. He laughed so loudly that a sleepy owl came out of a hole in a nearby tree to see what all the noise was about.

"Thank you, Mister Crocodile, for telling me where you are. I won't come near the water now." Feeling relieved that he had escaped again, but disappointed that there would be no crabs for breakfast, the jackal ran off to his house in the jungle.

The crocodile was furious. He was bigger than the jackal; he was stronger than the jackal; he was older than the jackal; and, of course, he was wiser than the jackal – or so he thought.

"I'm not going to let that jackal get away with tricking me twice," he thought, and he heaved his heavy body out of the water, up onto the riverbank, and off in the direction of the jackal's house. He hid himself in the jungle shadows close to the house, and then he waited.

It wasn't long before the jackal darted out of his house and took off into the jungle at a very fast pace – so fast he didn't even close the door behind him. He had to warn all his friends that the ferocious steel-jaw crocodile was still lurking in the river.

"Ho ho," thought the crocodile, "so you're going out. There may be a surprise for you when you come home again, and you won't be so clever this time." And he crawled

18

sluggishly up the path and through the door into the jackal's house.

The old croc waited and waited, smiling his crocodile smile each time he imagined how good the jackal would taste when he finally came home.

When the jackal finally returned, he was worried. His friends had been upset when he told them the bad news. "What are we going to do if we can't go to the river to drink, and to fish, and to wallow?" they had said. "What can we do to make the crocodile go away?" As the jackal walked toward his front door, he saw something that gave him an idea. But it also made him quiver with fear.

It was a trail that looked as if it had been made by a huge beast as it dragged itself along the path, right up to his front door.

"Could the crocodile be waiting for me inside my house?" he wondered. He had a plan, but first he had to be sure that the old croc was in there. The jackal stood boldly on the pathway and said in a loud voice,

"Hello, my little house. Is there something wrong? You haven't said 'Welcome Home' like you always do when I come home."

The crocodile, waiting under the kitchen table, heard this and snarled to himself. "All I have to do now is say 'Welcome Home,' and the jackal will walk right into my cunning trap." So, in the sweetest voice he could manage, the croc said, "Welcome home."

The jackal, in the calmest voice he could manage, replied, "I'm glad everything is fine. Thank you for welcoming me home. I will come inside when I've collected some wood for the fire."

The jackal moved like a flash. He collected lots of dry wood and very quickly piled it around the house. Then, quick as a flash again, he set fire to the wood!

The wood began to burn. The house began to burn. Wafts of smoke reached the croc's flaring nostrils and flames began to lick at his tough scaly tail. With a great despairing roar, the crocodile hurled himself through the jackal's front door and made for the river.

The jackal watched him go. The owl sleeping in the tree by the river woke up to see a great splash, as the old croc returned to

22

the river and swam away. And the ferocious steel-jaw crocodile was never seen in the jungle again.

The jackal's friends were so pleased that they built him a new house. And the jackal? Well, he never went without crabs for breakfast again.

THE BRILLIANT MIND

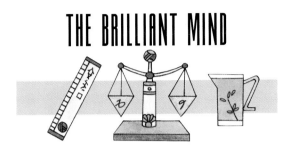

There once was a very clever woman, who lived with her husband Koyuri in a village in the foothills of Mount Fuji. Koyuri was a good man, but he was not as clever as his wife. Each day, he would go to her many times with questions. It didn't matter how difficult the questions were, Koyuri's wife would always find the answer. With this cleverness, Koyuri and his wife became rich.

Now, Koyuri was very proud of his wife, and he called her admiring names such as *Brilliant Mind, Wonderful Cleverness,* and *Precious Wisdom.* He wanted the whole village to know that their great prosperity was due to her. For many months he tried to think of a way to tell everyone of her cleverness.

At last, he decided what to do. He made a sign to hang on their door so that everyone who passed could read it. The sign said:

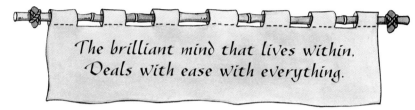

The brilliant mind that lives within, Deals with ease with everything.

Everyone in the village agreed that Koyuri was a very good man to praise his wife – she was an extremely clever woman.

One day a district official passed the house and read the sign. "What a vain and arrogant fellow lives there!" he thought. In fact, *he* was the vain and arrogant one. He didn't even know Koyuri or his wife, but he couldn't bear the thought of anyone being cleverer than himself. "I will punish him for making such a boastful claim," he muttered.

And, returning to his office, he sent a messenger to summon Koyuri before him.

Koyuri was very upset and confused by the summons. "Nothing like this has happened to me before – I'm a law-abiding citizen. Precious Wisdom, what have I done to deserve this summons?" he asked his wife despairingly.

26

Koyuri's wife was calm and unworried. "Do you know, I think the sign on the door must have angered the official," she said. "Go with the messenger now and you will soon find out if this is so. When you return, we shall decide what to do."

Feeling reassured, Koyuri went with the messenger. But as soon as he saw the official, he began to tremble with nervousness and fear. The district official sat behind a huge desk, and he glared at Koyuri as if he were ready to swat some nasty insect.

"So this is the wonderful fellow who puts up signs to tell of his own cleverness," he said, in such a loud, frightening voice that Koyuri could barely utter a squeak of protest. "You boast that no problem is too great for your brilliant mind, do you? Well, I have just three tasks for you. No doubt a mind as brilliant as yours will find them easy."

Koyuri bowed low and tried to speak, but the district official slammed his fist down on the desk.

"One!" he boomed. "You shall weave a cloth as long as a road."

"Two!" He slammed his fist on the desk again. "You shall produce as much rice wine as there is water in the ocean."

"And three!" Koyuri winced as he waited for the fist to hit the desk a third time. "You shall raise a pig as heavy as a mountain."

The district official looked very pleased with himself and continued in a voice of quiet arrogance.

"And if you don't complete these tasks by the third sunrise after the new moon, you will see what I think of your boasting!"

Koyuri bowed, and left in dismay. "Not even Wonderful Cleverness will be able to help me this time," he thought. "These tasks will take longer than a lifetime."

But Koyuri's wife only smiled calmly when he told her about the district official's impossible demands.

"There is a simple solution," she said. "The district official will see that your sign was not an idle boast." And she began to explain her plan to her husband.

The next morning, Koyuri went again to the district official. With him he took a ruler, a measuring jug, and a set of scales.

The district official was so surprised by Koyuri's quick return that he actually listened for once.

"Your Honor," said Koyuri. "I return to ask for further instructions."

"I was about to begin weaving, but I realized I needed to know the length of road before I could measure the cloth. So that you can measure the road, I have brought you this ruler.

"Also, I must know how much water there is in the ocean, so that I can be sure to make the right amount of rice wine. I have brought you this jug to measure the water.

"And, to know how big a pig to raise, I must know the weight of a mountain. To help you find this out, I have brought you this set of scales."

Koyuri took a deep breath and continued. "Once you provide me with each of these measurements, I will gladly begin the tasks you have set me." Then Koyuri bowed low to show his respect.

The district official frowned. He tried to appear sure of himself, but he was at a loss for words. He knew that it would take more than a lifetime to measure the length of a road, the water in the ocean, and the weight of a mountain.

Koyuri waited for what seemed like a lifetime and still the district official only frowned in silence. Then, at last, the district official almost smiled.

"You may go," he said. "And the tasks may wait."

Koyuri turned to go, and as he did, he was almost certain that he heard the district official murmur, "The sign on the door was true after all."

Koyuri rushed home and told his wife everything that had happened, and he and his Brilliant Mind lived happily ever after.

COLLETTE AND THE TREASURE CHEST

Once upon a time there lived a poor family: a man named Pierre, a woman named Marie, and their daughter, Collette. They lived in a small wooden house with a big old plum tree in the garden, and they had a cat named Claude. Marie worked hard sewing tapestries to sell at the market, and Pierre worked hard on a farm owned by the Mayor, who, in fact, owned almost all the land thereabouts and took care to pay his workers as little as he could.

During the day, Pierre and Marie worked without rest. Then, in the evenings, they met their friends in the village inn. They loved to talk and chatter about anything and everything that happened to them. Nothing was kept a secret. And if ever there was something interesting in their chatter, the whole village knew about it that very evening. Collette sometimes wished that her parents were not so talkative, but she loved them nonetheless and helped her family all she could.

One Saturday, Pierre and Marie were going to the next village to visit Marie's sister. Collette offered to go to the market to sell her mother's tapestries and buy some food. She took a short cut across one of the Mayor's farms, and on her way she tripped on something protruding from the ground. She stopped to see what it was.

Scrabbling around with her fingers, she uncovered an old chest, crumbling with age

and decay. Carefully she opened the lid. Out spilled shiny gold coins – the chest was full to the brim. She plunged her hands into the coins. Her family would be rich at last!

But this was the Mayor's land. He would try to claim the treasure for himself. She put a handful of coins into her pocket and quickly covered up the chest with earth and grass. She would keep the coins a secret from everyone, except her parents.

Then another thought occurred to Collette. Her parents would never keep the coins a secret. They would talk and chatter more excitedly than ever, and tell everyone at the village inn that evening. The Mayor would be sure to find out very soon after.

So Collette sat down in the field to think of a plan. It wasn't long before she had an idea. She went on to the market and sold all her mother's tapestries. Then, instead of buying the usual kinds of food, Collette bought a cackling brown hen, six eggs, and a sack of candy canes. Then she hurried home.

All over the plum tree in the garden she hung the candy canes. Then she collected all the plums from the tree, put them in a nest of straw by the back door, and sat the cackling brown hen on top. Last of all, she put the eggs in Claude's basket by the wood stove in the kitchen.

Just as she had finished, Collette saw her parents returning.

"Look at the plum tree!" exclaimed Pierre. "It's growing candy canes – what a treat!"

Marie was not so sure. "Where are all the plums? I won't be able to make plum jam."

"Don't worry about that," said Collette, leading them to the back door. "I bought a wonderful cackling brown hen at the market today – just look."

Pierre and Marie saw the cackling brown hen sitting on a nest piled full of plums.

"A hen that lays plums – what an amazing creature!" said Pierre.

"We will have plum jam after all," said Marie. "But it would have been nice to have some eggs."

"But we have eggs," said Collette. "Look in Claude's basket by the wood stove."

Marie and Pierre went into the kitchen, but all they saw was their cat curled up asleep in his basket. Collette put her hand underneath him and pulled out an egg. Pierre picked up the cat and they all saw five more eggs in the basket.

"This is wonderful!" Pierre shouted. "We must go to the village inn and tell everyone about all the amazing things that have happened to us."

"Indeed," said Marie, hopping from one foot to the other in her eagerness to be off. "We will go at once."

"Before you go," said Collette, "there is one other amazing thing to tell. Today, on my way to the market, I found a treasure chest, full to the brim with gold coins."

Pierre and Marie were so excited that they didn't wait to ask any questions. "We're rich! We're rich!" they shouted as they ran down the path toward the village inn.

As soon as they were out of sight, Collette collected the eggs, the plums, and the candy canes, and put them all in the kitchen.

It wasn't long before her mother and father returned. Their faces were red with shame and disappointment.

"How could you let us be so foolish?" said Pierre with his head in his hands.

"Everyone at the village inn laughed at us – they will never believe another word we say, and it's all because you played a silly trick on us," said Marie, almost in tears. "We can never go back to the inn again."

"But that need not concern you," said Collette, "because the last amazing thing was not part of the trick at all. I really did find a treasure chest of gold. We really *will* be rich."

"Then why did you trick us with the candy canes, the plums, and the eggs?" said Pierre.

"I had to make sure that no one found out about the treasure, so I made sure they wouldn't believe you if you told them," said Collette. And with that, she produced some gold coins from her pocket.

Pierre and Marie were delighted. Pierre gave a shout, and danced Marie and Collette around the room.

The next evening, instead of going to the village inn, Pierre and Marie went with Collette to dig up the treasure chest. Soon their cart was packed with all the family's belongings, including Claude and the cackling brown hen. And they all set off to find a new house, with a plum tree in the garden, where they could live happily ever after.

THE SHADY DEAL

In a very old city, in a very grand house, there once lived a very wealthy man. Outside his house, beside the road, grew a large magnolia tree. The wealthy man had planted the tree, and considered it to be truly his own.

One very hot day, a pedlar came along the road, carrying his heavy bundle of wares. The sun was beating down, and the pedlar was hot and tired. He stopped beneath the tree and sat down to rest in its cool shade. When the wealthy man saw the pedlar outside his house, he shouted angrily, "Why are you stopping here? Be off with you at once!"

"Why should I go?" protested the pedlar. "The roadside belongs to everyone, and I shall rest here just as long as I like."

"The roadside may very well belong to everyone," said the wealthy man, who was annoyed that the pedlar didn't obey him without question. "But you are using the tree, which *is* my property. I planted it, I watered it, and I am the only one who may enjoy its shade. Be off with you!"

The pedlar rose to his feet, but he made no further sign of leaving. "Well then, will you sell me the tree?" he asked.

Although the wealthy man was always keen to make more money, he merely laughed at such a suggestion. "There is not another tree for many miles. My tree is very valuable. Its price would be far beyond your purse," he said.

"True," said the pedlar calmly. "Perhaps then you would sell me the shadow that the tree casts? Surely that would not cost as much."

"Hmm," thought the wealthy man. "If the pedlar is foolish enough to wish to buy a shadow, then I am willing enough to sell one." And in a moment, he and the pedlar had settled on a price.

So the pedlar paid for the shadow of the tree. And the wealthy man, chuckling smugly to himself, drew up a deed of ownership and gave it to the pedlar.

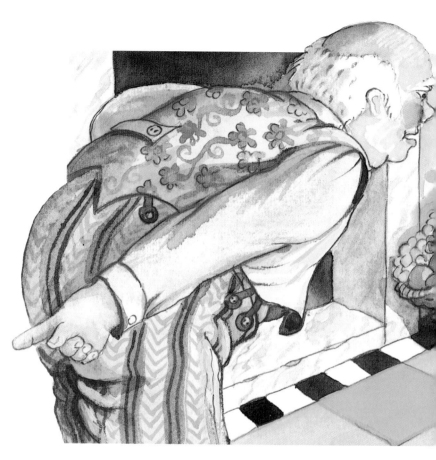

The next morning, the pedlar returned and sat in the shade of the magnolia tree. The sun slowly climbed in the sky, and as the shadow of the tree moved, the pedlar moved with it. By early afternoon, the pedlar had followed the shadow into the wealthy man's courtyard.

The wealthy man was furious. "How dare you trespass here!" he shouted. "Be off my land at once!"

But the pedlar only smiled and took the deed of ownership from the pocket of his ragged shirt. "Remember," he said, "you sold me the shade; I have the deed to prove it. And as I own the shade, I have the right to go wherever it goes."

Day after day the pedlar returned to sit in his shade. Sometimes he came alone. Sometimes he brought his friends to share

the coolness in the heat of the long, sunny, summer afternoons.

The wealthy man was so angry that he took the matter to court. But the deed proved beyond doubt that he had sold the shade, and the judge pronounced that the pedlar could indeed use it whenever he liked. But the wealthy man did not let the matter rest. He tried to buy the shade back. In desperation, he even offered ten times as much as the pedlar had paid. But the pedlar refused to sell at any price.

"The shade is very valuable," he said. "And it is not for sale. However, you may share my shade with me and with my friends whenever you like."

The wealthy man was so outraged that he packed his numerous belongings, and all his money, and left for another city.

And each day, as the hot sun beat down on the city, the pedlar and his friends enjoyed the magnolia tree's cool shade undisturbed.

TITLES IN THE SERIES